ALL ABOUT HORSES	6
BREEDS AND COLORING	8
HORSES IN THE WILD	10
BREEDING AND TRAINING	12
CARE AND EQUIPMENT	14
HORSES AT WORK	16
HORSES IN WAR	18
SPORTS FOR ALL	20
THE SPORT OF KINGS	22
THE ENTERTAINERS	24
HORSES IN HISTORY	26
HORSES IN MYTH	28
INDEX	29

First published in Great Britain 1977 by Ward Lock Ltd.
Copyright © 1977 by Grisewood & Dempsey Ltd.
All rights reserved. a b c d e f g h
This edition is published by Derrydale, a division of
Crown Publishers, Inc.
Printed in Singapore by Tien Wah Press (Pte) Ltd.

Library of Congress Cataloging in Publication Data

Justice, Jennifer L
   Let's look at horses & ponies.

   Includes index.
   SUMMARY: Introduces horses and ponies in the wild
and those used for work, sport, war, and entertainment.
Discusses their breeding, training, care, equipment,
history, and mythology.
   1. Horses--Juvenile literature. 2. Ponies--Juvenile
literature. [1. Horses. 2. Ponies] I. Bissex,
Thelma. II. Nockels, David. III. Thompson, Joan,
1943- IV. Title. V. Title: Horses & ponies.
SF302.J87 1979   636.1   79-84413
ISBN 0-517-287250

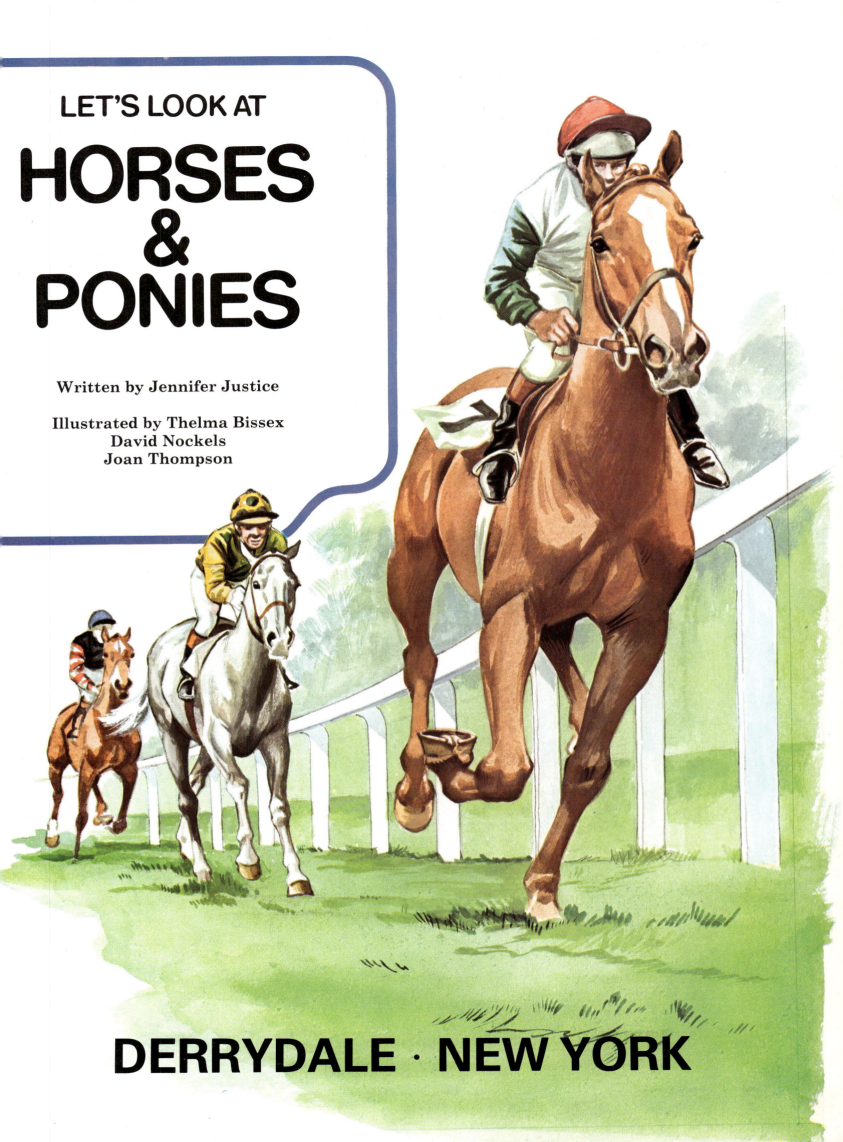

LET'S LOOK AT
HORSES & PONIES

Written by Jennifer Justice

Illustrated by Thelma Bissex
David Nockels
Joan Thompson

DERRYDALE · NEW YORK

All About Horses

Poll
Mane
Crest
Shoulder
Withers
Back
Haunch
Croup
Loins
Dock
Flank
Buttock
Thigh
Stifle
Gaskin
Hock
Fetlock
Hollow of Heel
Heel
Sheath
Ribs
Abdomen
Hoof
Forelock
Cheek Bone
Nostril
Throat
Chin Groove
Breast
Elbow
Knee
Cannon Bone
Pastern

It is important to know the "points" of a horse or pony when choosing an animal to buy. Here are some of the most important points, though there are many more. Horses and ponies are measured in "hands." A hand measures about 4 inches (10 cm). The measurement is taken from the ground to the highest point of the withers. A horse stands at a height of 14 hands 2 inches (14.2 hands) or more. A pony is 14.2 hands and under.

The horse has been a friend to Man for thousands of years. Ever since the wild horse was first tamed, horses have played an important part in history. They have worked as pack animals, carrying heavy loads. They have pulled plows and wagons. Many horses have carried soldiers into battle.

Horses have also taken part in many sports. The Ancient Romans used horses in their chariot races. In Asia, tough, sturdy ponies were used to play polo. Today we still keep horses for pleasure – not just to ride, but for hunting, racing, show-jumping, and circus acts.

When buying a horse or a pony it is important to know what to look for. The horse's eyes and ears should show alertness. Its back should be nice and straight and not "hollow." The horse's legs should be firm and straight; its hindquarters should be strong. It is always a good idea to get the advice of a vet before choosing a horse or pony to buy.

THE FIRST HORSES
About 55 million years ago, a fox-sized animal called *Eohippus* (dawn horse) lived in North America. It ran on slender "fingers" and "toes."

By the time *Mesohippus* (middle horse) came along, the middle toe on each foot had grown bigger and the outside toes had begun to shrink.

Merychippus looked more like a modern horse, with four large, curved hooves. But it stood only about 40 inches (100 cm) high.

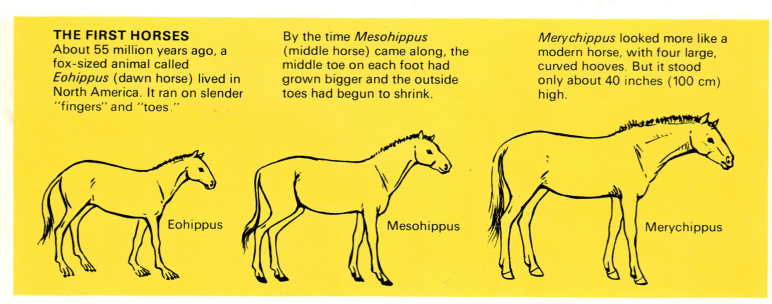

Eohippus
Mesohippus
Merychippus

All animals that have a single hoofed toe on each of their four legs belong to the horse family. The relatives of the horse include donkeys, mules, zebras, onagers, and, of course, wild horses.

Donkeys are smaller than horses. In many parts of the world donkeys have been used for centuries to carry heavy loads. A male donkey, or jackass, and a female horse, or mare, can be mated to produce a mule. A mule is bigger than a donkey, and is a strong and hard worker.

Zebras are really a type of wild ass. Their stripes help to hide them from enemies on the African plains. Another sort of wild ass is the onager.

The quagga once lived in southern Africa. It was partly striped, like a zebra. But quaggas were hunted for their meat, and today there are none left.

HOW A HORSE MOVES

Walk To walk, a horse raises its feet one after another. Walking has a four-beat rhythm.

Trot Trotting is a faster pace than walking. It follows a two-beat rhythm.

Canter The canter has a three-beat rhythm.

Gallop Like walking, the gallop has a four-beat rhythm but is much faster.

Breeds and Coloring

Horses and ponies come in many different breeds and colors. Each type of coloring has a special name. For example, a reddish-brown horse is called a chestnut. A bay is a brown horse with a black mane, tail and legs. Grays have a mixture of black and white hair. Sometimes horses have large patches of black or brown and white hair. They are said to be piebald or skewbald. Palominos have beautiful golden-brown coats with white manes and tails.

Below are some of the different types of face markings:

blaze

snip

star

baldface

dun

brown

strawberry roan

bay

palomino

piebald

chestnut

skewbald

gray

black

Icelandic pony

Shetland pony

Appaloosa

Welsh cob

Thoroughbred

Arab

This page shows some of the many breeds of horse and pony. Ponies are all under 14.2 hands high and there are many separate pony breeds. The smallest member of the horse family, usually found in Britain, is the Shetland pony. A full grown Shetland stands only about 3½ feet (a meter) high. The biggest horses are Shires, one of the group of "heavy horses," as these powerful work horses are called.

Lipizzaner

Quarter Horse

Morgan

Breton

Shire

Horses in the Wild

There is only one true wild horse left in the world today: Przewalski's horse, which lives in Mongolia. But there are still many horses that live in the wild in different parts of the world. They come from tame horses that once lived with Man but returned to the wild.

The Wild Mustangs

Mustangs are small, sturdy and cunning wild horses that live in the West. The ancestors of these horses were brought to America by Spanish explorers about 500 years ago. Before Europeans came to the New World there were no horses living here. When the Spanish first arrived in Mexico with their horses, they frightened the Indians that were living there. Never had the Indians seen such monsters. They thought that the men on horseback were gods with the head of a man and the body of an animal. Soon the Indians lost their fear of horses and began to make use of them. Mounted Indian warriors of the Plains became master horsemen (see page 18).

Mustangs can be a variety of colors. They are very independent animals, and can be difficult to tame.

Camargue horses wade through shallow marsh waters. They are sturdy and can survive the harsh conditions of life in the Camargue region.

Wild Horses of the Sea

In the southern part of France there is a large, marshy region called the Camargue. For hundreds of years herds of small, tough horses have roamed this region, grazing on the rough marsh grasses. Known as Camargue horses, they are only partly wild. Each year some of these horses are rounded up by French "cowboys" called *Gardiens*. They are used by the *Gardiens* to herd black bulls that are raised in the Camargue and used for bullfighting. Tame Camargue horses also carry tourists through the marshes to look at the beautiful flocks of flamingoes that live there.

Przewalski's horse is the only true wild horse living today. Named after the man who discovered the breed, this small horse lives on the Mongolian plains. It looks a bit like a grayish-brown donkey. Today there are very few Przewalski's horses left in the wild, but a number are kept in zoos.

Breeding and Training

A mare, or female horse, carries her foal for about 11 months before it is born. The foal can stand up on its wobbly legs a few minutes after it is born. It can begin to run around in only a few hours. A foal has very long legs compared to the size of its body.

The mare feeds her foal with milk from her body until the foal is about six or seven months old. Even before this the foal will begin to nibble at grass. A male foal is called a colt after it is a month or two old. A female is called a filly. At one year, a colt is about half grown. Most horses do not reach their full height and weight until they are five years old. But mares can begin to have foals at the age of three or four.

Training a horse starts as early as possible. A foal should be handled from birth and introduced to a headcollar at an early age. The age at which a horse or pony is "broken in," or trained for riding, depends on its breed and what it will be used for. Generally, three years is the best age.

chestnut mare and foal

lungeing

Lungeing

A horse or pony must be trained, or "schooled," before it makes a good riding animal. One type of training exercise is called lungeing. The trainer moves the horse around him in a circle on a long lunge rein. The trainer puts the horse through all its paces, using his voice and a whip as aids.

Lungeing helps to train the horse to move quietly in a circle, first at a walk or trot, then at a canter. It also gets him used to commands of the voice.

Starting to Jump

Horses and ponies jump naturally even when they are not being ridden. Even so, there are important exercises that help rider and horse to learn to jump together. The first step in learning to jump is simply walking and trotting over poles laid flat on the ground about 4 to 6 feet ($1\frac{1}{2}$ to 2 meters) apart. The next stage is jumping over "cavalletti." These are long poles attached to "X"-shaped wooden supports. The height of the poles can be changed just by turning the "X" over on the ground. Later on, cavalletti can be stacked to make even higher and broader jumps.

Riding a circle teaches a horse to move evenly and obediently.

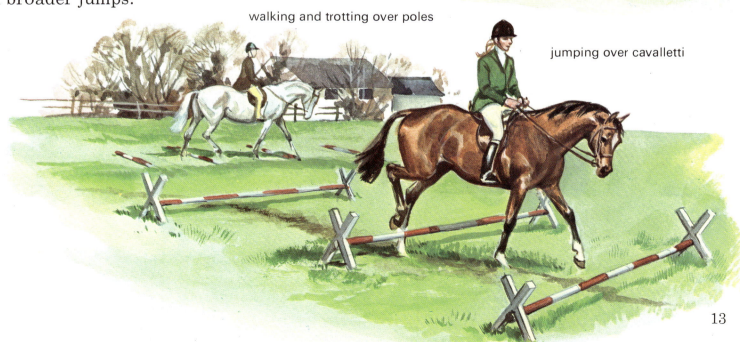

walking and trotting over poles

jumping over cavalletti

Care and Equipment

A horse's saddle, bridle, bit and girth are all part of the equipment called "tack." Safe riding means using the right sort of tack correctly and keeping it in good order.

The saddle fits on the horse's back to make it easier and more comfortable to ride. Attached to the saddle are the stirrup leathers. These are the strips of leather that hold the stirrup irons. There are several different types of stirrup iron. The one shown in the picture at the right is called a Plain Hunting Iron, and is the one most commonly used. The girth holds the saddle firmly in place. The girth buckles must be tightened both before and after the rider has mounted. It is very important that a saddle fits a horse or pony exactly.

The bridle and bit, with the reins, are for controlling the horse. A horse's mouth is very soft and it is important to be gentle when using the reins.

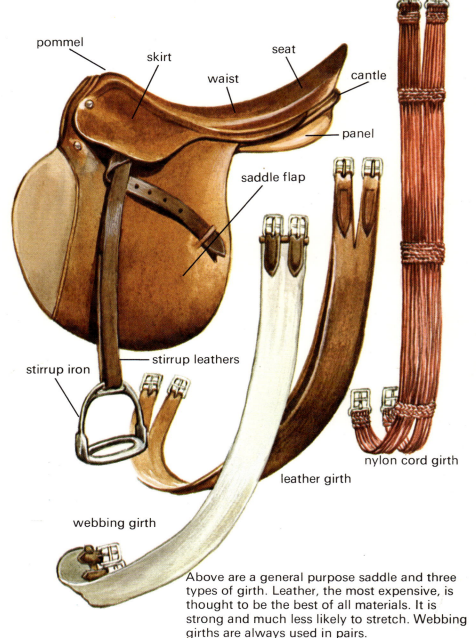

pommel / skirt / seat / waist / cantle / panel / saddle flap / stirrup leathers / stirrup iron / webbing girth / leather girth / nylon cord girth

Above are a general purpose saddle and three types of girth. Leather, the most expensive, is thought to be the best of all materials. It is strong and much less likely to stretch. Webbing girths are always used in pairs.

BRIDLES AND BITS

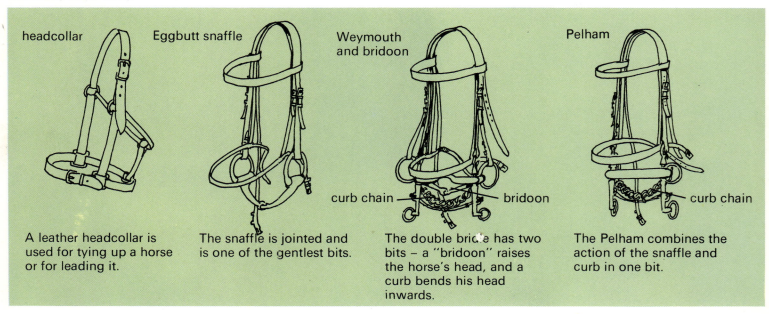

headcollar   Eggbutt snaffle   Weymouth and bridoon   Pelham

curb chain   bridoon   curb chain

A leather headcollar is used for tying up a horse or for leading it.

The snaffle is jointed and is one of the gentlest bits.

The double bridle has two bits – a "bridoon" raises the horse's head, and a curb bends his head inwards.

The Pelham combines the action of the snaffle and curb in one bit.

Grooming and proper care of tack are very important. Below are some things you will need.

GROOMING

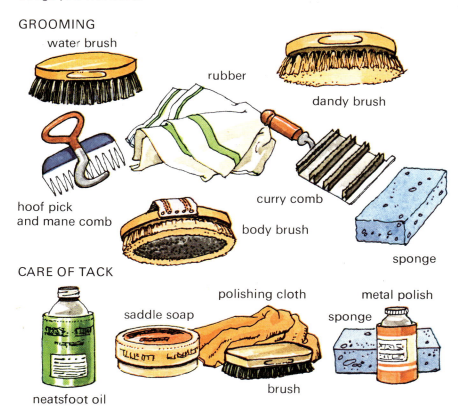

water brush

rubber

dandy brush

hoof pick and mane comb

curry comb

body brush

sponge

CARE OF TACK

neatsfoot oil

saddle soap

polishing cloth

brush

metal polish

sponge

Looking after a horse or pony is an important part of horsemanship. Horses not only need feeding, but they must be groomed and cared for.

A horse that is kept out at grass is the easiest to keep, providing he is well fenced in and there is plenty of grass and fresh water for him. A horse that is kept in a stable is more difficult to look after. He needs regular feeds, grooming and clean bedding. He must also be exercised every day.

Providing fresh bedding is an important part of looking after a horse. In the picture below, all the soiled straw has been removed. The rest of the straw has been tossed to one side to air, and the floor is being swept clean. The boy is bringing in fresh straw to replace what has been removed. At night the horse will need plenty of straw for bedding. Behind the horse hangs his hay net, filled with hay for him to eat. At the right is a full bucket of fresh water.

Horses at Work

Horses have been working for Man ever since they were first tamed. Because they are strong and easy to train, horses are used for many jobs. They can pull or carry heavy loads. Even today, the amount of work done by a machine is sometimes measured in "horse-power." Horses are also excellent animals for herding cattle and sheep.

police horse

pit pony

coal cart

Pit Ponies

Small, sturdy ponies were once used in coal mines to pull carts filled with coal. Called pit ponies, they were harnessed to the cart, which ran on rails like a train. The ponies lived in stables underground for months at a time. They only saw daylight when they were brought up for a "holiday" on a farm.

Working with the Police

Horses have been replaced by machines for many types of work. But today the police horse is still an important worker. In many countries policemen on horseback patrol city streets and help to control crowds.

Shire horses

Australian stockmen

In the picture above, stockmen round up cattle in Australia. When they are not working, stockmen enjoy taking part in rodeos very like those in North America. These rodeos include an event called "buckjumping," which is like bronco busting, as well as bullock riding.

On the Range

Cowboys are not just a feature of the American West. Today, in North and South America, Australia and New Zealand, horses are used by modern "cowboys" to herd cattle and sheep. An Australian herder is called a stockman. He rides an Australian Stock Horse, which is a mixture of breeds. Australian Stock Horses are also good stadium-jumpers, eventers and polo ponies.

The cowboys of South America are called *gauchos*. They ride mustangs to round up huge herds of long-horned cattle.

gaucho

When Indians wore full war paint and feathers, their ponies often did too. Each painted marking had a special meaning.

Horses in War

Before men learned to ride they discovered that horses could be trained to pull chariots. In Ancient Assyria chariots were an important part of the army. They were drawn by teams of two or more horses. The horses were trained to charge when commanded by the driver and urged on with a whip. Later, in Ancient Rome, charioteers competed with one another in races at special arenas called "circuses". Sometimes sharp blades were fixed to the chariot wheels. These could do a great deal of damage to the other chariots in the race.

Indian Ponies

Some of the most skillful mounted warriors in the world were the Indians of the Great Plains. They caught and tamed many of the horses first introduced to America by the Spaniards.

Indian ponies were small and tough. The Indians often rode them bareback. They controlled their mounts with their legs, leaving both hands free to handle their weapons. While riding at full gallop, a warrior could even slide down to fire from underneath his horse's neck, while protected by its body.

Roman charioteer

Warriors of the East

The fierce and warlike Mongols of the steppes of Asia were expert horsemen. They rode small but sturdy Mongolian ponies, fighting on horseback in much the same way as the North American Indians. Their ponies were trained to stop and turn quickly during their lightning attacks.

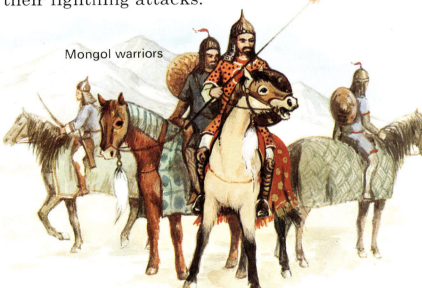

Mongol warriors

knight in armor

Knights in Armor

One of the best known mounted warriors in history was the knight of the Middle Ages. The horses that the knights rode were very big and heavy, rather like the "heavy" breeds of today. They had to be strong enough to carry the knight fully armed and dressed in a suit of armor. Sometimes even the horse wore armor to protect its head and neck. Knights and their horses took part in tournaments, where they fought mock battles to test their skill and courage.

Gun and Cannon

In the early 1800s the French Emperor Napoleon set out to conquer Europe. His army and those of his enemies included large groups of cavalry, as mounted soldiers are called. Cavalry horses were trained to be obedient even when surrounded by smoke and the noise of gun and cannon fire.

Napoleon's cavalry

19

Sports for All

Horses have been used for sport for thousands of years. Many of these sports began as a form of practice for fighting, as in the game of polo. The hunt grew out of the farmers' need to get rid of animal pests. These sports help to improve the skills of both horse and rider.

Stadium-jumping is a popular sport. Millions of spectators enjoy watching it live or on television. There are many different types of jumps, including fences, walls and water jumps. The best jumpers have lots of courage and like to jump. Some horses jump record heights in the "Puissance," or high jump.

Dressage is a French word that means "schooling" or "training." It is actually a very advanced form of the ordinary schooling of a horse. In dressage the rider must pay attention to even the smallest detail. Each of the horse's movements must be accurate and controlled, and the horse and rider must move smoothly together. A dressage test includes different paces and turns. Each rider is marked on how smoothly and accurately his horse goes through the movements. The judges watch carefully to see how quickly the horse obeys its rider's instructions.

stadium-jumping

Polo is an exciting sport that was first played over 2000 years ago in Asia. It was brought to Europe from India in the 1800s. In polo, two teams of players on horseback try to drive a wooden ball through their opponents' goal posts. They use a wooden mallet with a long handle to hit the ball. Polo horses are specially trained to move, turn and stop quickly. They must also get used to having polo sticks swung close to their heads. They wear special leg boots or bandages to protect them from the swinging polo sticks.

polo

cross country

Eventing is a competition that includes dressage, show-jumping and cross country. In a cross country course horse and rider must cover a route that includes many difficult natural fences.

Hunting is a very old sport. Riders wear special clothes and follow certain rules. Their horses must be strong and intelligent. They are specially trained for the sort of countryside they will hunt.

hunting

The Sport of Kings

Horse racing is one of the oldest sports in the world. It is sometimes called the "sport of kings" because many kings bred racehorses and took part in watching them compete. The Thoroughbred is the best type of racehorse. All Thoroughbreds are descended from three Arab stallions brought to Britain by King Charles II. They were called Byerley Turk, Darley Arabian and Godolphin Barb. Today the rules of racing as laid down by the Jockey Club are accepted throughout the world.

steeplechasing

Jockeys wear colorful shirts and caps called silks. Each jockey wears the colors of the horse's owner, so that the spectators at the race can recognize them easily.

There are several different kinds of horse racing. Flat races are run on grass or dirt tracks. People bet money on which horse is going to win. The distance of a race is measured in "furlongs." A furlong equals $\frac{1}{8}$ of a mile.

Before the race the horses are paraded around the paddock. Here the owner or trainer has a final word with the jockey, who will ride the horse in the race. Then all the horses and riders move into the stalls of the starting gates. The starter presses a button which opens the gates and rings a bell. The horses are off!

Steeplechasing is an exciting race that includes jumps over fences. It gets its name from races once held across fields in Ireland. Those taking part set their course between the church steeple of one village and the next. This kind of racing became known as "steeplechasing." In the modern steeplechase there is a limit of 12 fences in the first two miles and 6 fences in each additional mile. The Grand National in Britain is a famous steeplechase.

owner

jockey

trainer

paddock

harness racing

Harness racing is a popular sport in the United States and is becoming popular in many other parts of the world. In some countries harness racing includes "trotting" or "pacing." Horses that are used in harness racing are specially bred for speed.

flat racing

Horses pound the turf on the homeward stretch of a flat race. Jockeys must be small and light, so that the horses can move faster. They crouch, standing in the stirrups. And they lean as far forward as they can to help the balance of their horses.

The Entertainers

The word rodeo comes from a Spanish word that means "round-up." Rodeos began over 100 years ago. Cowboys got together to show off all the skills they used when breaking in horses and herding cattle. Rodeos soon grew into colorful spectacles with many special events. These include bareback riding, in which a rider must stay on a bucking horse for at least 10 seconds. He rides without saddle or reins. Saddle-bronc riding is like bareback riding except that the cowboy uses a saddle, halter and one rein.

The bareback rider is a daring performer. Not only must he stay on the bucking horse, he must also use his spurs to encourage the horse to kick and buck even harder.

bareback rider

bucking bronco

circus horse

Under the Big Top

For hundreds of years horses have been star circus performers. Some of the most famous circus horses are Liberty horses. These are often pure or part Arab. They are highly trained to carry out graceful "ballets" in the circus ring. Other circus horses are trained to canter smoothly around the ring while bareback riders perform various feats on their backs.

Lipizzaner

Bull riding is a daring event in which a cowboy rides bareback on a bull for at least 8 seconds. He holds on to a rope that has been looped around the bull's body.

Calf roping is done while riding. The cowboy must throw a rope around a running calf, then dismount, throw the calf to the ground and tie three of its feet. An expert rider can do this in as little as 12 seconds.

"High School" for Horses

White Lipizzaner stallions are famous throughout the world for their spectacular displays. They are trained at the 400-year-old Spanish Riding School in Vienna, a "high school" for horses. Lipizzaners are schooled for three to five years to be expert, controlled performers. The name *Lipizzaner* comes from the town of Lipizza in Yugoslavia where they were first bred.

Horses in History

Horses have played an important part in history. Many explorers, soldiers and other great heroes have had horses that helped them to carry out their deeds.

One of the most famous horses in history was made of wood. About 3500 years ago, the Ancient Greeks attacked the city of Troy in Asia Minor. They built a huge wooden horse and left it outside the gates of Troy. The Trojans thought the horse was sacred and would protect them. They dragged the horse through the gates and into the city. But late that night, when all the Trojans were asleep, a small band of Greek soldiers crept out of the horse. They opened the city gates for the rest of the Greek army, which rushed in and captured the city.

Alexander the Great

Bucephalus

Trojan horse

Conqueror of the World

Alexander the Great was a ruler of Greece and one of the greatest generals in history. He conquered a huge empire that stretched from the Mediterranean Sea to India. Even when Alexander was young he was brave and fearless. He tamed the beautiful horse Bucephalus, which no one else dared to ride. Bucephalus carried Alexander on his long journeys. When the horse died, Alexander built a city called Bucephala in its memory.

The Emperor's Horse

One of the most pampered horses in history was Incitatus, the favorite horse of the Roman Emperor Caligula. Incitatus was kept in an ivory stall in a marble stable and wore a jeweled collar. Its blankets were dyed purple, the color of royalty. It was said by some people that Caligula had even made his horse consul, a very high rank in Roman government!

Caligula

Incitatus

Napoleon

Marengo

Great War Horses

The French Emperor Napoleon's horse Marengo was a gray Arab stallion. The horse was named after a famous battle that Napoleon's army fought and won. After Napoleon's defeat at Waterloo, Marengo was brought to Britain. His skeleton can be seen today at the National Army Museum in London.

General Robert E. Lee led the Confederate Army during the American Civil War. His horse, Traveller, was a big gray, part Thoroughbred, part Morgan. Traveller fought many battles with Lee and was never wounded. The horse was Lee's constant companion until the general's death.

Robert E. Lee

Traveller

Horses in Myth

Many horses and horse-like beasts have become famous as characters in myths and legends. The unicorn, whose name means "single horn," was a popular mythical animal in the Middle Ages. People believed it had special powers. The unicorn is often shown as a white horse with one long, spiral horn on its forehead.

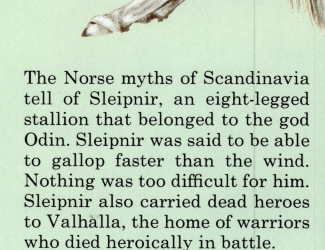

unicorn

Pegasus

The Norse myths of Scandinavia tell of Sleipnir, an eight-legged stallion that belonged to the god Odin. Sleipnir was said to be able to gallop faster than the wind. Nothing was too difficult for him. Sleipnir also carried dead heroes to Valhalla, the home of warriors who died heroically in battle.

Pegasus was a mythical winged horse of ancient Greek legend. He was said to have been tamed by Bellerophon, with the help of a golden bridle given to him by the goddess Athena. Today one of the Constellations, or star clusters, is named after Pegasus.

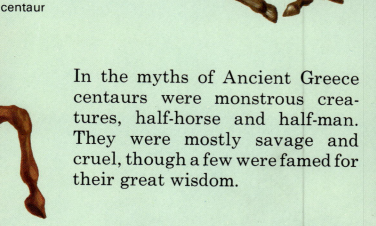

Sleipnir

centaur

In the myths of Ancient Greece centaurs were monstrous creatures, half-horse and half-man. They were mostly savage and cruel, though a few were famed for their great wisdom.

Index

A
Alexander the Great 26
American Indians 10, 18
Ancient Greeks 26, 27
Ancient Romans 6, 18, 27
appaloosa 9
arab 9, 22, 25, 27
armor 19

B
baldface 8
bareback riding 18, 25
bay 8
bit 14
blaze 8
"breaking in" 12, 13
breeds 9, 17, 22, 23
breton 9
bridle 14
bridoon 14
bronco 17
Bucephalus 26
bucking 24
buckjumping 17
bull riding 25
buying a horse 6

C
calf roping 25
Caligula 27
Camargue horses 11
canter 7
cavalletti 13
cavalry 19
centaur 28
chariots 6, 18
chestnut 8
circuses 18, 25
colt 12
cowboys 11, 17, 24, 25
cross-country 21
curb 14

D–E
donkey 7
dressage 20
dun 8
Eohippus 6
eventing 17, 21

F
filly 12
flat racing 22
foal 12
furlong 22

G
gallop 7
gardiens 11
gauchos 17
girth 14
Grand National 22
gray 8, 27
grooming 15

H
hands (height) 6, 9
harness 16
harness racing 23
headcollar 12, 14
heavy horses 9
hooves 6, 7
horsepower 16
horse racing 22
hunting 20, 21

I–J
Icelandic pony 9
Incitatus 27
jackass 7
jockey 22
Jockey Club 22
jumping 13, 17, 20, 22

K–L
knights 19
Lee, General Robert E. 27
Liberty horses 25
Lippizaner 9, 25
lungeing 13

M–O
mare 7, 12
Marengo 27
markings 8
Mesohippus 6
Merychippus 6
Mongol warriors 19
Morgan, 9, 27
mule 7
mustangs 10, 17
Napoleon 19, 27
onager 7

P
pack animals 6
paddock 22
palomino 8
Pegasus 28
Pelham bit 14
piebald 8
pit ponies 16
points of a horse 6
police horses 16
polo 6, 17, 20, 21
Przewalski's horse 7, 10, 11

Q–R
quagga 7
quarter horse 9
racehorses 22
riding a circle 13
riding exercises 13
rodeo 17, 24

S
saddle 14
saddle-bronc riding 24
schooling 13, 20, 25
Shetland pony 9
shire horse 9, 16
silks 22
skewbald 8
Sleipnir 28
snaffle bit 14
snip 8
spurs 24
stable 15
stadium-jumping 17, 20
stallion 22, 25, 27
star 8
steeplechasing 22
stirrups 14, 23
stockmen 17
strawberry roan 8

T–U
tack 14
thoroughbred 9, 22, 27
tournaments 19
trainer 13, 22
Traveller 27
Trojan horse 26
trot 7
unicorn 28

W–Z
walk 7
war paint 18
warriors 10, 18, 19
Welsh cob 9
Weymouth 14
wild ass 7
wild horses 7, 10, 11
zebra 7